FLUTE MUSIC OF THE BAROQUE

for Flute and Piano

Selected, Revised and Annotated by Louis Moyse

G. SCHIRMER, Inc.

DISTRIBUTED BY

HAL•LEONARD®
7777 W. BLUEMOUND RD. P.O. BOX 13819 MILWAUKEE, WI 53213

Contents

		Piano	Flute
KARL PHILIPP EMANUEL BACH	Allegro from: *Concerto in A Major*	26	10
LUIGI BOCCHERINI	Allegro moderato from: *Concerto in D Major, Op. 27*	3	2
FREDERICK THE GREAT	Sonata XI in D minor	38	13
ANDRÉ E. M. GRÉTRY	Allegro from: *Concerto in C Major*	14	6
JEAN MARIE LECLAIR	Adagio from: *Concerto in C Major Op. 7, No. 3*	80	28
JEAN-BAPTISTE LOEILLET	Adagio and Gigue from: *Sonata in G Major*	121	41
JOHANN CHRISTOPH PEPUSCH	Sonata in F Major	124	42
GIOVANNI BATISTA PERGOLESI	Allegro spiritoso from: *Concerto in G Major*	113	38
GIOVANNI PLATTI	Sonata II in G Major	53	18
JOHANN JOACHIM QUANTZ	Arioso from: *Concerto in G Major*	21	8
KARL STAMITZ	Concerto in G Major	64	22
GUISEPPE TARTINI	Concerto in G Major	84	29
ANTONIO VIVALDI	Concerto in D Major (*Il Cardellino*) Op. 10, No. 3	98	33

Allegro moderato
from: Concerto in D Major, Op. 27

Luigi Boccherini
(1743-1805)

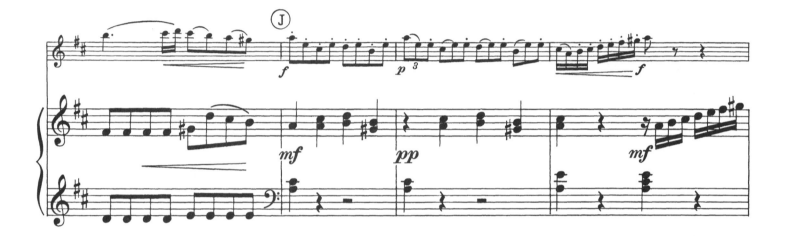

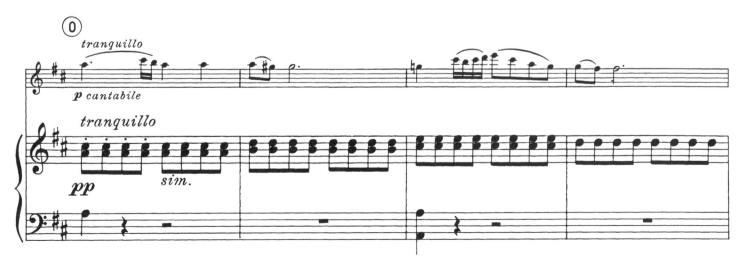

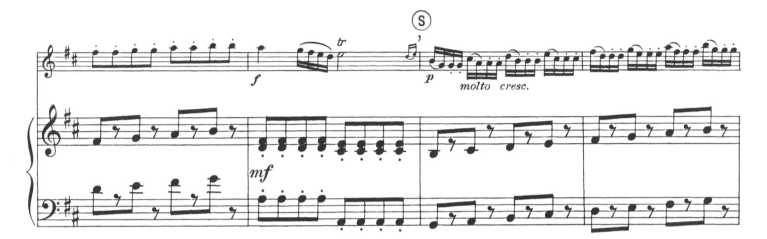

Allegro

from: Concerto in C Major

André E. M. Grétry
(1741- 1813)

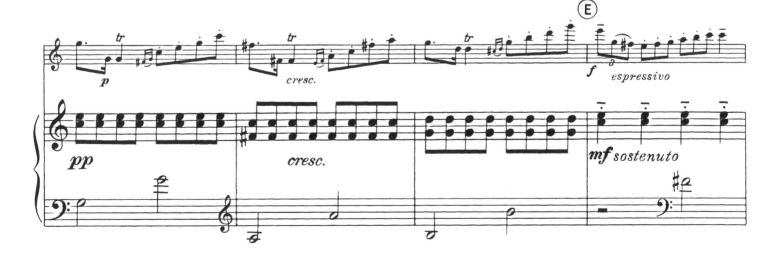

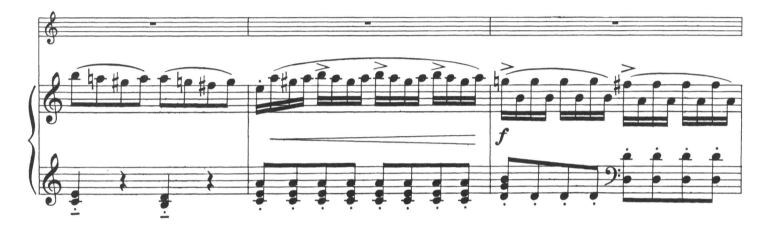

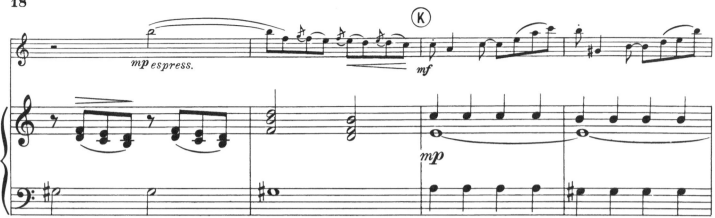

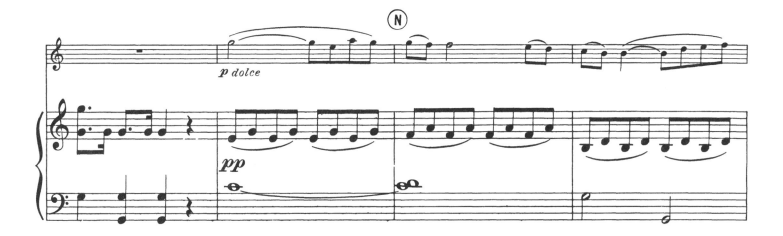

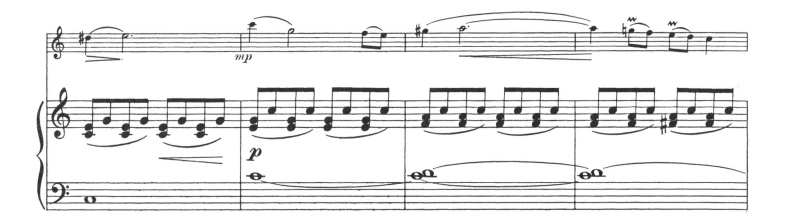

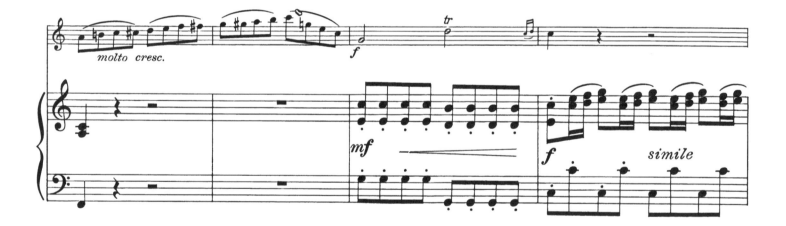

Arioso

from: Concerto in G Major

Johann Joachim Quantz
(1697-1773)

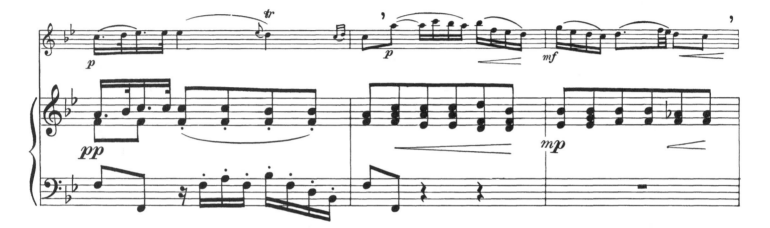

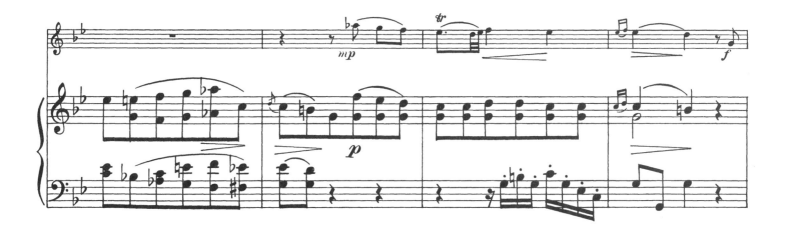

Allegro
from: Concerto in A Major

Karl Philipp Emanuel Bach
(1714-1788)

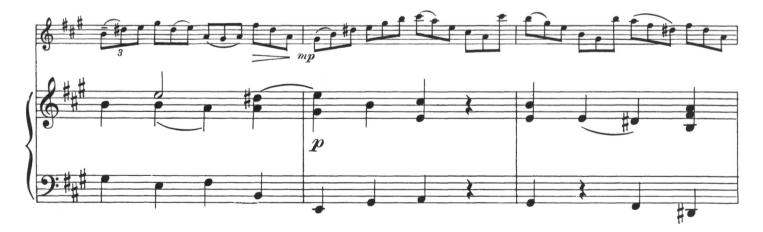

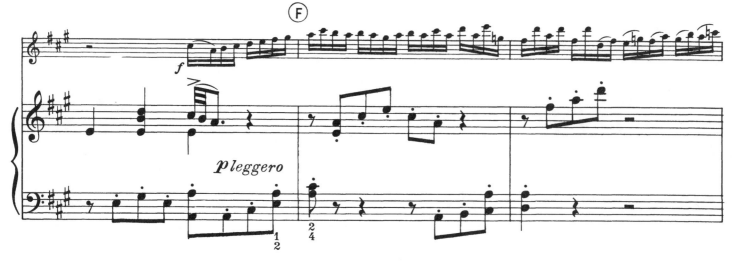

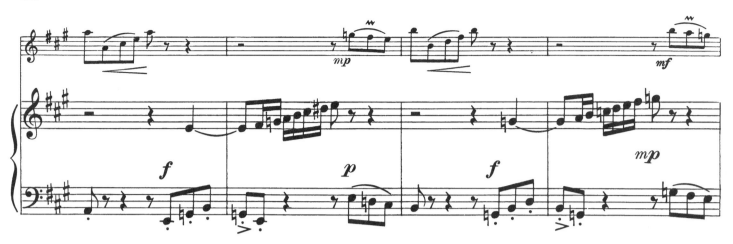

Sonata XI in D minor

Frederick the Great
(1712-1786)

I

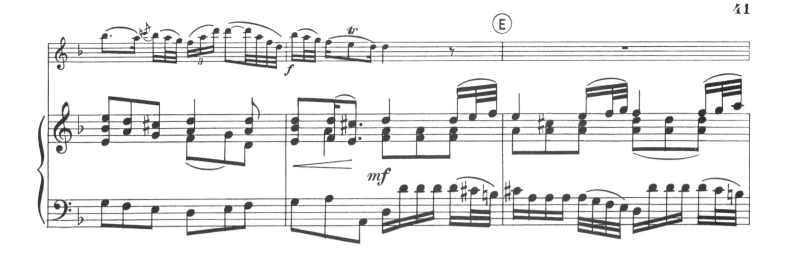

II

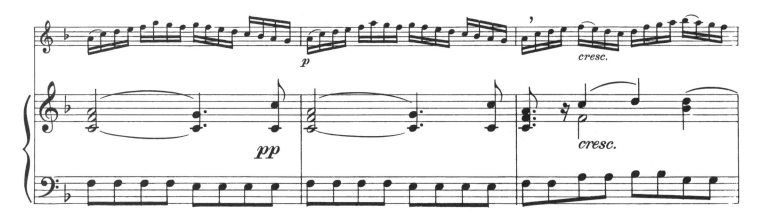

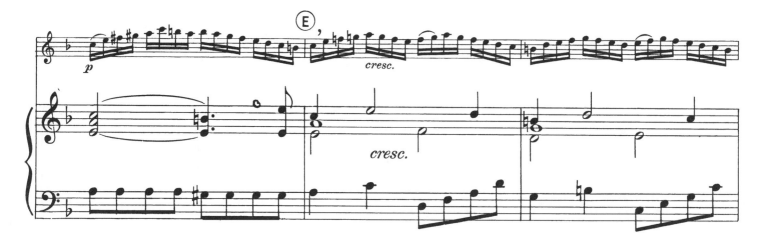

III

Sonata II in G Major

Giovanni Platti
(1690-1763)

I

II

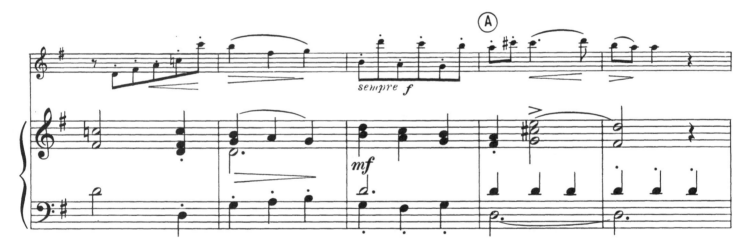

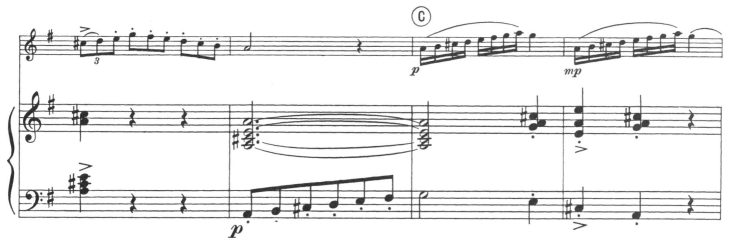

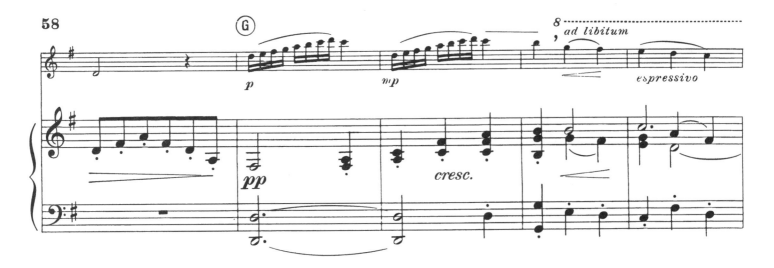

Adagio

IV

Concerto in G Major

I

Karl Stamitz
(1745-1801)

Allegro moderato

II

Andante poco adagio

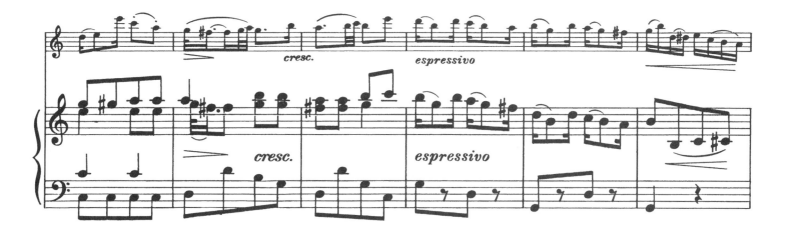

III

Adagio
from: Concerto in C Major

Jean Marie Leclair, Op. 7, No. 3
(1697–1764)

Adagio

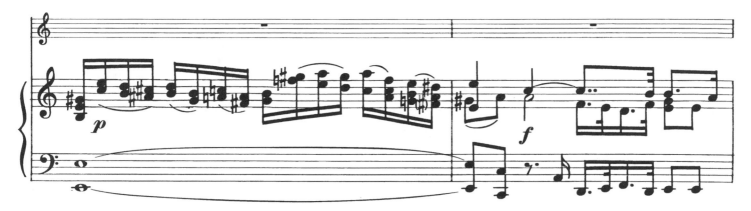

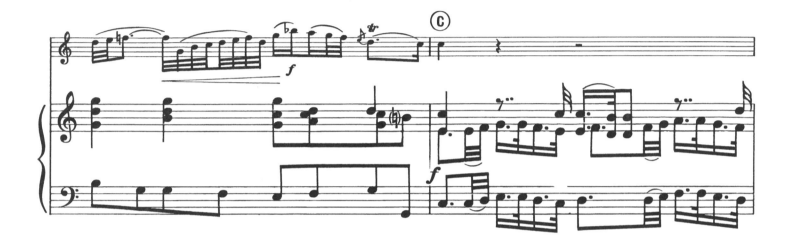

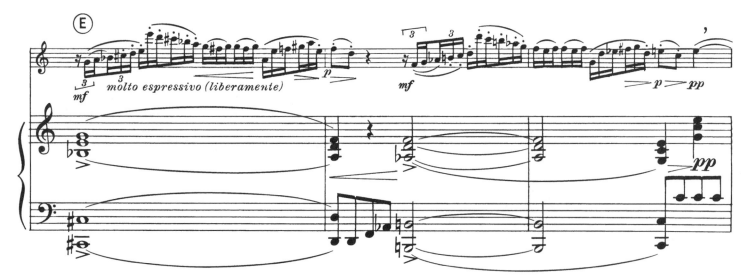

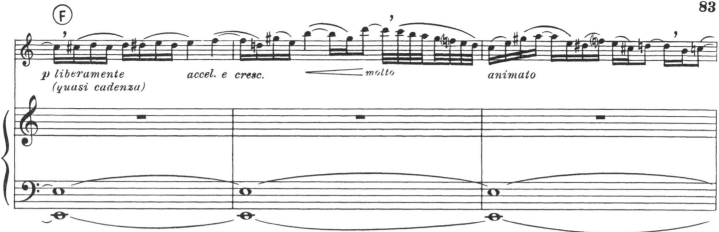

Concerto in G Major

Guiseppe Tartini
(1692-1770)

I

Allegro non molto

II

Andante

III

Allegro

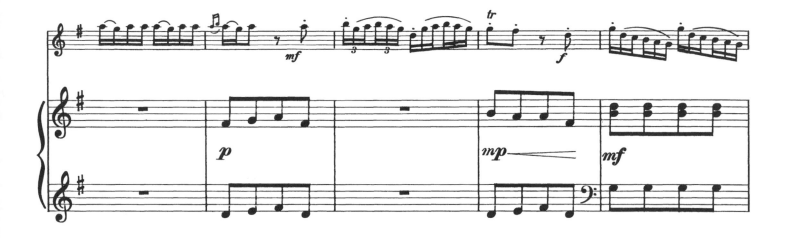

Concerto in D Major
Il Cardellíno

Antonio Vivaldi Op. 10, No. 3
(1669? - 1741)

I

Allegro

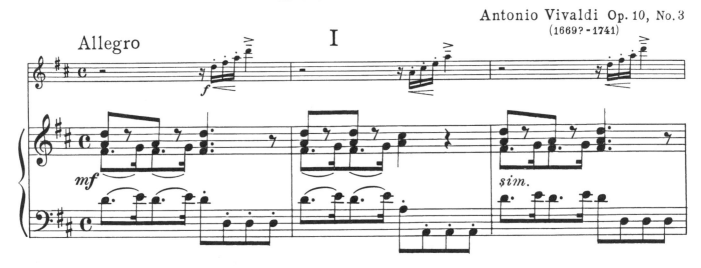

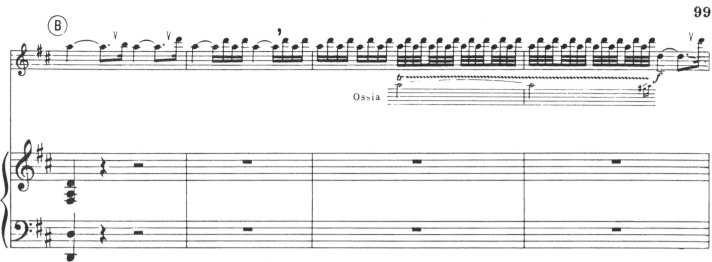

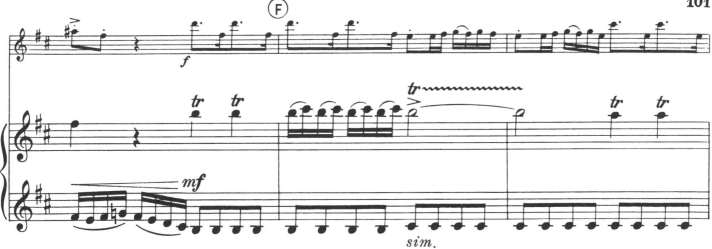

II

III

Allegro spiritoso

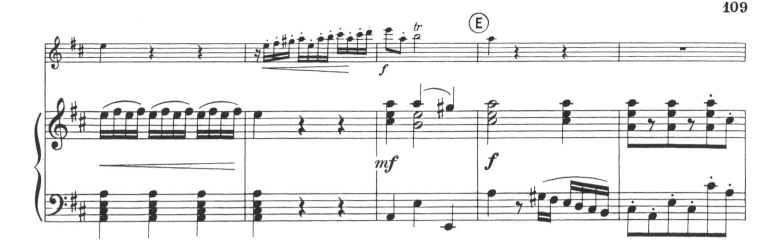

Allegro spiritoso

from: Concerto in G Major

Giovanni Batista Pergolesi
(1710 - 1735)

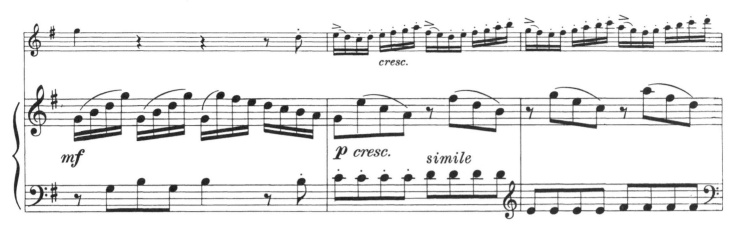

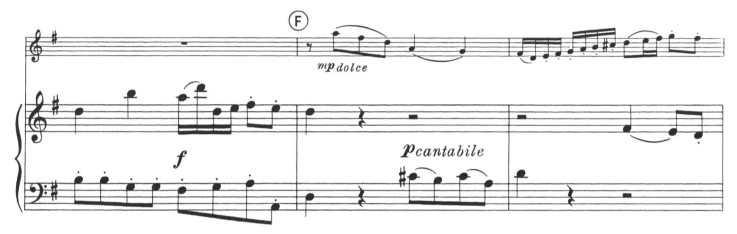

Adagio and Gigue
from: Sonata in G Major

Jean-Baptiste Loeillet
(1680 - 1730)

Adagio

Gigue

Sonata in F Major

Johann Christoph Pepusch
(1667-1752)

I

II

Allegro

III

IV